Prairie Christmas

Written by Elizabeth Van Steenwyk
Illustrated by Ronald Himler

Eerdmans Books for Young Readers
Grand Rapids, Michigan • Cambridge, U.K.

Text © 2006 Elizabeth Van Steenwyk
Illustrations © 2006 Ronald Himler
Published in 2006 by Eerdmans Books for Young Readers
An imprint of Wm. B. Eerdmans Publishing Company
2140 Oak Industrial Drive NE, Grand Rapids, Michigan 49505
P.O. Box 163, Cambridge CB3 9PU U.K.

www.eerdmans.com/youngreaders

Manufactured in China

07 08 09 10 11   8 7 6 5 4 3 2

Library of Congress Cataloging-in-Publication Data

Van Steenwyk, Elizabeth
Prairie Christmas / written by Elizabeth Van Steenwyk ; illustrated by Ronald Himler.
p. cm.
Summary: On the Nebraska prairie in 1880, eleven-year-old Emma finds a way to
celebrate the spirit of Christmas while her mother, a doctor, delivers a baby on Christmas Eve.

ISBN-10: 0-8028-5280-7 (alk. paper)
ISBN-13: 978-0-8028-5280-9 (alk. paper)

[1. Christmas — Fiction. 2. Mothers and daughters — Fiction 3. Doctors — Fiction.
4. Prairies — Fiction.] I. Himler, Ronald, ill. II. Title.
PZ7.V358Pr 2006
[E] — dc22
2004009869

The display type is set in Lo-Type.
The text type is set in Saxaphone.
The illustrations were created with pencil and watercolor.
Gayle Brown, Art Director
Matthew Van Zomeren, Graphic Designer

For Kedrin, with love
— *E. A. V.*

For Paul, in friendship
— *R. H.*

A knock on the door wakes me in the night. I listen as Mama opens it.

"I'm John Cooper, a neighbor of the Van Der Meers," a man says. "They say to hurry because their baby is coming."

"It's too soon." I hear the worry in Mama's voice as she closes the door.

Mama always goes when someone comes to tell her she's needed. And I always go with her because she won't let me stay home alone. Mama's a doctor, and she says it's about time women got to be doctors. After all, it's 1880.

But why does she have to be a doctor tonight? Christmas Day has just begun and the two of us had our own plans. Now Mama will be working and I'll be waiting, just as though it's any other day.

She goes out to the barn and hitches Old Dan to the buggy. I follow and feel crisp, bright air on my cheeks. Gran knit a woolly scarf for me when I was a baby, and tonight I wrap it closer to my chin. It used to be miles too long, but little by little I'm growing into it now that I'm almost eleven.

Mama tucks our Texas Star quilt around us, then Old Dan takes off on the dirt road that heads north through Nebraska. The jingle of bells on his bridle announces that we're coming, and a bright star shows the way.

"Come on, Old Dan," Mama says. "We can't be slowpokes tonight."

One hour later, we pull into the barnyard. Mr. Van Der Meer opens the front door even before Old Dan's bells have stopped jingling. "Hurry," he says.

The Van Der Meers' house and barn are built under one roof. The animals live on one side, the family on the other. The animals can look right into the great room through the half-open doors.

Mr. Van Der Meer and Mama rush into the house. I unhitch Old Dan and give him a measure of oats in his nosebag before following them.

A lamp brightens one corner of the great room and a mantel clock strikes two as we step inside. A small, undecorated fir tree stands nearby. Christmas was interrupted here, too.

Logs sputter in the fireplace, throwing off a warm glow. I am drawn to it, while Mama wraps herself in a white apron.

"She's asking for you," Mr. Van Der Meer says.

Mama nods and follows him into another room to tend to his wife.

Now comes the waiting part, but I'll never get used to it. In the rocking chair beside the fire, I wrap my thick scarf around me and doze until the clock strikes again. I waken and realize that I am being watched.

Two little faces peer at me from the sleeping cupboard in the wall. In their night clothes, they look like frightened angels.

"Is our new baby here yet?" the little boy asks. He comes to stand close to me.

"No," I say. "It might take a while." Most of my Christmas, I add to myself.

His sister is tall, and her braids are long. "What's your name?" she asks.

"Emma. What's yours?"

"Hansie," she answers. "My brother is Will."

A low groan from their mother comes from the bedroom. Hansie and Will look alarmed and step closer to each other.

"Don't be afraid," I tell them. They're not having much of a Christmas either.

Will helps himself to an apple from a wooden bowl on the table, and Old Dan begins to shake his head.

"Old Dan likes apples, too," I say, and take one to him.

While his giant jaws crunch the apple, I stroke his long, silver mane. He's always liked that. Then I get an idea.

"What are you doing?" Hansie asks.

"Watch."

I comb my hands through Old Dan's mane and loosen strands of hair. Then I gather a handful and give some to Hansie and some to Will.

"What shall we do now?" he asks.

I go to the tree and begin to hang the silver threads on its branches. They do the same.

Mr. Van Der Meer bursts in from the bedroom. His hair stands up like dry straw, and his shirt collar is wrinkled. "A towel. I am to get a towel." He looks at us as if we are strangers.

I find one near the wash basin. He takes it and rushes back to the bedroom. Unanswered questions — mine, Hansie's, and Will's — hover around me.

Will puts his hand in mine and looks at me. "I want my mama," he begins.

So do I, I think. But I am older so I do not say that aloud. I can spare a hug though. It's good for him and for me as well.

"I'm hungry," Hansie announces. "Ma didn't feel like making supper last night." She glances at the bedroom door, anxious and uncertain.

"Let's make breakfast," I say. Their faces brighten.

"You?" Will asks.

"Me," I say. "When my mama's tired, I cook."

I go to the cupboard and find rice and cinnamon and sugar and salt and raisins, too.

"Porridge," Hansie cries.

"Christmas porridge," I correct her.

She helps me coax a fire in the stove. Soon the rice is bubbling in the pan and the scent of cinnamon floats everywhere.

We hear more alarming sounds from the bedroom.

"Why don't we sing?" I ask quickly. "Do you know 'Silent Night'?" They try to follow along but don't seem to know the words.

We grow restless in our waiting. The clock sounds another hour. Hansie finds bits of bright yarn to tie on the tree. Will adds his papa's shiny cigar wrappers. I find a few red berries in a bowl and tuck them here and there on the branches.

A knock on the door interrupts us, and I go to open it.

Mr. Cooper stands there, fingers of dawn streaking the sky behind him. "The light from the lamp has been glowing all night. We've been worried," he says.

He holds a large plate of cookies and steps inside, followed by two other neighbors. One man carries a small goat. The other holds two lambs.

"The baby is not here yet," I tell them.

"Not yet?" Mr. Cooper questions. "But it has been so long . . ."

We look at one another. How much longer will we wait?

I pass the cookies and we eat in silence. Will reaches for another. The neighbors pull out chairs at the table and sit. I resume my place in the rocking chair and Hansie crowds in beside me. Will plops on my lap. The chair creaks in rhythm with the clock.

"I'm glad you're here, Emma," Hansie whispers. "I didn't think we were going to have Christmas until you came."

And then we hear it — a baby's soft cry.

"He's here!" Will shouts. "He's here!"

All of us, the children, the visitors, and I leap up together and rejoice in laughter and tears and hugs. Will drops the cookie plate but no one minds.

Soon the bedroom door opens, and Mama comes out. She looks tired, and I remind myself to do the dishes all by myself tonight.

She speaks to Hansie and Will. "Your pa is bringing the baby and your ma in here where it's warmer."

She saves a special smile for me.

They come, Mrs. Van Der Meer walking
slowly and carefully. She sits in the
rocking chair and takes the baby from
her husband. The blanket that wraps the
newborn is threadbare from two other
babies. Old Dan hears the commotion and
looks on from the half-open doors. A cow
and a donkey join him.

Mr. Cooper and the men step forward to
offer their gifts to the baby, a goat for milk
and lambs for wool.

It is a night for gifts. Hansie and Will give apples, and I hand my long scarf to Mrs. Van Der Meer. She wraps it around and around her newborn. The baby will grow into its miles of warmth, as I did, and one day outgrow it, as I have done tonight.

Later after everyone has eaten Christmas porridge,
Mama and I hitch Old Dan to the buggy and drive home
in a scattering of soft and silent snow.

"I'll always remember this Christmas," I say. "Always."